Behind THESE Closed Doors:

An Account in Poetry
by Someone You Thought You Knew

Michelle Carter-Douglass

BEHIND THESE CLOSED DOORS:
An Account in Poetry by Someone You Thought You Knew
ANNIVERSARY EDITION
© 2005, 2007, 2017, 2018 Michelle Carter-Douglass

ISBN 9781731400017

Tres Luces Publishing dba WCD Professional Services OHIO
Tres Luces Publishing is committed to finding a focus on solutions to epidemics that plague our communities. Through art and literature, we strive to bring awareness and alternative solutions for the stressors of our world today.

Book Formatting and set-up designed by Michelle Carter-Douglass of Wilson & Clark Professional Services LLC

The author(s) are available for motivational speaking and all speaking engagements. Please refer your interest in booking individual and or group appearances by calling (330) 881-3434.

Authors written works are also found on Amazon.com

All scripture references are taken from The King James Version Holy Bible and unedited.

I would like to thank The Almighty God for, loving me. Heavenly Father, I praise you. So many times, I thought I could not go forward in life. You brought me and my children out of homelessness. You have ordered our steps and protected us. Thank you, Heavenly Father.

Dedication

I would like to dedicate this book to my children, mother, sister, niece, aunts, and uncles.

I love you all for being there right by my side through all the hard times.

MCD

To My Little Girl, Kailah Mychelle Douglass,

We love and miss you with all our hearts. I long for the day, I will hold you in my arms and won't have to let you go.

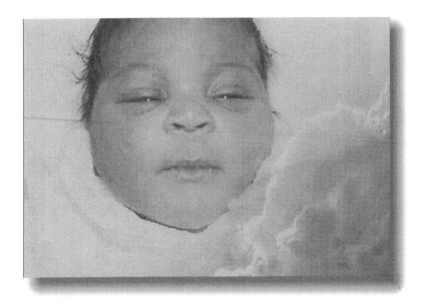

Gratitude

I would like to thank my children: Patrick M. Douglass, Arlessa R. Douglass, Brialan M. Douglass, and Kailah M. Douglass. I love you guys so much. Everything I do is for you. Thank you, guys, for believing in me.

I would like to thank my mother for helping me raise my children. Mommy, you do so much for me and my babies. You are a true blessing from The Heavenly Father. Thank you for pushing me to get this project done.

Lastly, I would like to thank my aunts, uncles, sister, niece, and cousins. My niece, Patrice Henderson. My sister, Nicole Carter. My aunts: Irma Casey, Darlene Culver, Warnetta Millhouse, and Frances Wilson. My uncles: John Wilson, Jerome Wilson, and Cortland Casey.

Dear Reader and Friend,

In writing my poetry, I will not use fixed English. I will capitalize words referencing to The Almighty God. This is my way to show respect to our Heavenly Father.

I will also replace pronouns with numbers. Example being, two (2) and four (4). Misspellings and other misuses of grammar are intentional and part of my specific writing style.

The following poems are a collection of memoirs beginning from the year 2004 to present. At another time, I plan to share four other poetry books.

1. **Behind Closed Doors:** A collection of Poetry by someone you thought you knew.
2. **Broken Mirrors & Mended Wounds**
3. **Poetic Intimacy**
4. **In Light**
5. **In Darkness**

With gratitude,

Michelle Carter-Douglass
MCD

Illustrations/Photographs by:

Patrick M. Douglass

Brialan M. Douglass

Arlessa R-N Douglass

Table of Contents

Introduction of King Paper
& Queen Pen   **39**

CHAPTER TWO
The Emergence of Michelle Denise   **53**

THE BONUS CHAPTER
Selected written works   **72**

Reader N Friend,

Watch my written words become wings.

I now, with poetry have my lock to this key.

4 many years and scores;

I have remained Behind Closed Doors.

Memoirs

&

Ardors

From Monroe Street 2 Spiritual Mansions

Who would have thought?

Two little girls born to Patricia Anne,

Would come up grand.

Both daughters,

individually educated and strong.

Both daughters,

spiritually committed to our God.

Reflecting back in memory,

it seems like only yesterday.

Mama was getting ready for work,

for she had to put food on the table and bills to pay.

As my sister and I were home from school,

Mom just finished her meal of fried chicken and lima beans.

Who would have thought years later,

I would be able to empathize with mother.

Patricia Anne Wilson Carter is one of the greatest mothers.

Mommy, I now can appreciate.

Momma, I value your encouraging words and hard work.

On Monroe Street, right across from the corner store,

the Campbell Jet is where we resided but did not stay.

This was not our spiritual residence.

Nonetheless, it was only our physical resting place.

Mommy always said her daughter would have more.

Our mother said to wait 4 the opening of The Lord's door.

However, mommy with you my sister and I already had more.

Who would have thought?

Two little girls born to Patricia Anne,

Would come up grand.

Both daughters,

individually educated and strong.

Both daughters,

spiritually committed to our God.

Reflection flash of past,

whoa, it seems like only yesterday.

Father God,

why in my mind am I stuck on this page in my life.

The taunts of my corrective shoes.

The scoffs of my mother's single parenting.

Silly, simple and idle people,

we poor people, too have dreams.

No longer wearing corrective shoes Boo.

The single mother had strong parents and siblings too.

See it is the village of the Wilson and Clark that raised these kids.

Close your eyes and in envision me to you saying this,

"it was the teachings of the village that allowed me to forgive.

The bitterness of yesterday gone I send you this tender sweet kiss.

Reader and friend,

forgiveness is a bliss.

Go ahead send your haters a tender kiss.

Reader, family, and friends,

isn't forgiveness an infinities bliss?

Little sister and niece,

this climb to do better in life,

I like. I like.

Little cousin,

this page of poetic forgiveness.

I like. I like.

For continued success, we strive.

My beautiful daughters,

this climb to do better in life,

I like. I like.

My handsome sons,

this page of poetic forgiveness.

I like. I like.

For continued success, we strive.

Who would have thought?

Two little girls born to Patricia Anne,

Would come up grand.

Both daughters,

individually educated and strong.

Both daughters,

spiritually committed to our God.

Mommy taught me from wrong and right.

I give a thankful sigh.

My momma was taught by her mom.

I sing my grandmother a thankful song.

Her mother was taught from her momma and so on.

I thank The Almighty Lord for a family unit so strong.

Biological, DNA father had to leave our lives, little sister.

Our mother was a domestic violence survivor.

Her daddy and brothers are her earthly protectors.

I write to my grandfather gracious words.

I write to my uncles, "thank you" in poetic words.

I am thanking our Gracious and Sovereign Lord.

Who would have thought?
Two little girls abandoned by Earl James,
Would come up grand.
Both daughters,
individually educated and strong.
Both daughters,
spiritually committed to our God.

My aunts,
this climb to do better in life,
I like. I like.
Little cousins,
this page of poetic forgiveness.
I like. I like.

For continued success, we strive.

From Monroe Street 119.5,

I climb to this spiritual mansion of growth.

With continued striving for success,

I find this taste soooooo sweet as it satisfies.

Momma's single parenting skills have no background laughter now.

Gratitude to those who embrace the rumors and untruths.

The Heavenly Father is shining on both you and me.

Who would have thought?

Two little girls born to Patricia Anne,

Would come up grand.

Both daughters,

individually educated and strong.

Both daughters,

spiritually committed to our God.

MCD

aka Monroe Street

A Letter 2 God

Dear Father,

So many days, have I remained lost?
Father,
So many days I have been lost.

My days have come and gone.
My heart has grown fierce and strong.
Yet, my mind and spirit sometimes are beaten down.

Father,
You have been there for me.
I love You, for You are my reigning King.
I greatly appreciate you abundantly.

As my spirit and heart endures these seasons,
my God,
with my spirit, you have seasoned me again and again.
Amen, say all of the men.

My spirit in time shall possess that perfected seasoning.
Amen, say all of the men.

Father God, your will shall prevail again and again.

Amen, say all of the men.

Though days have come and gone.

I can feel man bitterness frost unthaw.

OOOOOoooo say ahhhhhhh.

Cheers to new days and seasons blessed from Allah.

Though days have come and gone,

my heart grows patient and strong.

My mind and spirit in line with God.

Cheers to this new seasoning spiced from Allah.

Father,

you have been there for me.

I love and thank you.

I 4ever need and desire to serve you.

Humbly,

MCD

To My Little Dougies,

I love you more than words can describe. I know sometimes people make another feel inferior. It is the darkness and unhappiness in them. You continue shining so bright in life.

Love,

Mom

-

The Ticking of my clock

So many things in life I am destined to do.

Yet, time refuses for me to be still.

wishful pause

My eyes are opened to new things.

I still believe there can be a change among man.

a wave with my wishful wand

Mirror, I desire to see a change in this personal reflection.

This change and step, mirror reflection,

I must make this step before more time runs out.

wishful pause

This alteration of self-declared.

This step-in change is what the present is about.

I write this self-change in poetry.

Reader and friend witness this change with thee.

MCD

Arlessa Reign: Here we go—here we are

To reign, Miss. Lady, "I and era or time in which someone such as a king or a queen rules a nation." (Merriam Webster Online Dictionary)

Arlessa you have ruled even in my womb. There were times I did not want to press forward. I thank you for blessing me with your presence. Others look up to you. Your kindness is a blessing to many. You are talented, beautiful and smart.

When you were younger, you overcame much ignorance. This was the foolishness of others and the idle work of the enemy. The Lord has always had a plan for you. Keep your head held high and shine! None can ever dim a star. Shine Arlessa. Shine so bright as The Lord watches you from on High.

With Love,

Mommy (Michelle Denise)

P.S. I am so sorry I ate your Icey honey bun in the refrigerator.

Brialan aka Bright Eyes

You are so caring and intelligent. Brialan, you have the ability to go so far in life. Your heart loves so quickly and it is easy for others to wound you. I know this, my son because this used to be I.

Your eyes speak volumes son. Matthew 6:22-23 reads, "your eyes are a bright lamp — leading to goodness." "Everyone has a purpose." Proverbs 19:21 At times, a purpose can be accomplished at a young age in a short amount of time. Brialan from conception your mission was accomplished. You helped my heart and spirit in so many ways.

You do not need to be a football star nor a millionaire. You do not need to have blue eyes or a lighter shade of skin. You are an image of God. Your reflection shines as bright as the universe stars.

My storms in life were calmed once I held you in my arms. There is a calming spiritual flow each time I look into your eyes. I was blessed with you, your brother and sisters in life.

Remember no person can dim a star. Shine Brialan Matthew. Shine so bright!

With love,

Mom
Michelle Denise

Patrick M. Douglass aka First Born

It wasn't too long ago when I gave you some advice. I said take a deep breath. Allow only kindness and empathy to exhale.

I knew you were a blessing in my womb. The night I felt you kick for the very first time; I felt alive. Some thought you would never read or right. Some thought you would never speak (*yeah right*).

Now in awe, they sit there with mouths opened wide. Compelled to take in your wisdom. Graduated high school and so intelligent and bright.

Always remember you are the better part of your father.
I want you to know you are the greatest part of me. Keep
your head held high, First Born.

Know that none can dim a star. So, continue to shine.
Continue to be a joy in my life always.

Love Mom,

Michelle Denise

To My Children

Kailah Douglass,

Patrick Douglass, Arlessa Douglass, and Brialan Douglass

I love you all more than words can define. You kids have taught
me to forgive. The process of growing is hard. So many times, I

29

thought about giving up. I am so honored, that The Almighty God, sent me four angles.

I am so proud of you young adults. My daughter in Heaven, I cannot wait to hold you in my arms again. I love you all so much.

In my womb,

all four of you babies should grow.

I once thought I could protect you all.

Never did I think I would let one of my babies go.

In my heart, I hold you all close.

In my spirit, you all give me growth.

Can I say "I LOVE YOU," again and again?

I as a mother but have only one wish,

continue to hold on to God's Loving Hands.

Kailah Mychelle Douglass
AKA Baby Kay/Angel Girl

I miss you so much. I pray and still call out your name. I pray and hope that one day, Heaven will show mercy and bring you back to me.

I remember that day. I bathed and dressed you my little one. You smiled up at me. If only tears and grief would bring you back to me.

I never had the strength to leave your earthly father. I miss your smile. I miss holding you in my arms. I want you here so much. If only tears would bring you back to your earthly family. Kailah. Come back to us PLEASE!!!

We want you here so much. When the sun shines, it's as if you are smiling down on me. On my porch to you baby girl, I sing lullabies. When the blows as I sing the course, the wind blows a kiss upon me. My little girl is telling her mommy, "hello." Know you are our shining star. Mommy's gonna hold you again on that going home faithful day.

Love Mommy,

Michelle Denise

Spiritual Engagement

Memoirs 2

our Lord

Epiphany of me

I look back on my pictures in life.

Why?

Gratitude 2 my Heavenly Father and my earthly mother.

Sigh

The devil wore a disguise.

He whispered that there was no love 4 I.

Lies.

LIES.

ALL LIES!!!

My dearest friends said, "know your worth."

My dearest friends ignored the rumors and lies.

Thank you.

Thank you 4 being true in the midst of my storms.

Heavenly Father,

Thank You ever sooooo graciously.

I thank You, Heavenly Father 4 loving me,

4 blessing me,

4 my babies and,

4 my friend and family.

Opened doors.

Unbroken Relationship

I am guilty of letting go of Your Hand so many times.

So, guilty of not feeding my spirit, my heart, and mind.

I. I, I, I. I am broken, Father.

This spiritual soul is held captive.

Guilty of taking for granted Your Everlasting Life Line.

When things go bad,

I go to a hiding place.

Shaking My Head in Distaste.

When my life encountered something bad,

I go into this dark, dark place.

A house can come and go.

My life, my children belong to You.

A house can come and go.

My life, my sobriety belongs to You.

NO car; I will walk.

NO house; My Lord, You Shelter.

Hold me
Protect me
Console me
Chasten me; 4 eternity.

At the age of forty-three,

You brought me so far.

Father God, I never genuinely showed gratitude 2 Thee.

This sedated character, now in the forgiveness stage.

Thank You, Heavenly Father; Love MCD.

Now aged cuarenta y tres (43),

I a longer road to travel.

On the road to do what is just.

The avenue of In Servitude, I am now traveling.

At the age of forty-three,

Father, King Paper& Queen Pen; walk with me.

Aged Cuarenta y tres,

Father God, Prince Patrick, and Prince Brialan; come run with me.

God of Abraham, Princesses Arlessa & Kailah; come to walk then run with me.

A house can come and go.

The road to In Servitude; I travel earnestly.

Padre Dios; I genuinely Thank Thee.

My sedated character; forgiving.

Gracias.

Hold me

Protect me

Console me

Chasten me; for eternity.

With Love,

MCD

New Found Praise

Oh, sweet children of The Highest God:
Know your beauty and know your worth.

The enemy wants to blind our hearts and distort our
minds.

The crafty want to place malice in the kindest of hearts.

The lowly almost took the better part of Michelle Denise.

Do you feel that you are not pretty enough?
Are you tired and spiritually bruised?
Reader & Friend . . .
I am too.
Do you think you are not intelligent like the rest?
Do you feel sometimes you are taking your last breath?
Reader & Friend . . .
I had those same feelings too.

Stand Up!

Stand up and whisper our Savior's Name.

Tell the idle worker, we are no hostage for his game.

Male & Female Soldiers of The Lord:

Through Christ, we are Re-born and know our worth.

I am guilty of unkind words.

I at one time had malice inside my heart.

With Jehovah, I have been cleaned.

Depression, negative thinking, animosity:

In Jesus Christ's name 'Sit Down!'

Brother and Sisters Get up.

Brothers and sisters,
Open your eyes to the skies above.
See the clouds?
Do you see the tars at night?
Up above, or God is watching you and me.

Too skinny.

Too fat.

Too dark.

Too light.

This is the devil's talk.

Hair too short.

Hair too long.

Hair too straight.

Hair too kinky.

This is the devil's chatter.

I am somebody.

The Heavenly Father completed me.

God's stitching began in your mother's womb.

(Psalm 139:13) KJV

Oh, sweet women and men of The Highest God,

Know your loveliness and your value.

The enemy wants to blind your eyes.

The sly want to place malice in your hearts.

Do you feel that you are not handsome enough?

Are you weary and battered?

I am too.

This is the idle work of the lowly.

Get up.

Stand up.

Remain Prayed Up.

Introduction of
King Paper & Queen Pen

2 My Readers and Friends

A Home Built from Commiserated Love

Tonight, my heart beats for all in this world.

My heart beats for you, you and you too.

I am praying for those in pain this night.

I am praying for those that have been told lies.

Reader, Friend and those residing on this earth,

The Lord hears our cries.

Writer's sigh . . .

I know what it feels to love and to hate.

I know what it means to be cold at night and day.

If I could—I would shelter you.

I would shelter you with commiserated love.

To anyone that has been hurt,

Whether it was physically, mentally or emotionally,

may God, build you up spiritually.

Father God,

The tears from my soul begin to flow.

In this poem, shall heal my soul.

King Paper,

on this table, I have placed you.

Father God,

the tears from my soul oh, how they flow.

From this poem, I shall heal my soul.

King Paper,

meet our Ruler.

Queen Pen.

I recognize how it feels to love and to hate.

I see what it means to be cold at night and day.

If I could—I would shelter you.

I would shelter you with commiserated love.

To anyone that has been hurt,

Whether it was physically, mentally or emotionally,

may God, build you up spiritually.

Father God, in our Lord and Savior
Jesus Christ's Name—Build them up!!! Amen

Humbly,

MCD

*T*o *W*hom *I*t *M*ay *C*oncern,

Dear Reader and Friend, this poem in epistle form, I let you in. I open all of my windows and thus my doors. Please come in and have a seat.

As I close my eyes.

I bow my head humbly down.

King Paper and Queen Pen have taken their place.

To Insecurity,

I no longer eat at the same table. Through God's words, I am growing more spiritually, mentally and emotionally enabled. By the words of God's angels, I am breaking free. I am breaking free from the jealous and simple.

The image in the mirror; I can see without animosity. I am in love with my skin, eyes and embrace my obesity. My work is a true gift from HE. Our God is with me. So, in the next line, I say goodbye to insecurity.

With love,
Michelle Denise

Dear Abuser,

I no longer despise you.
In looking back,
I can now say,
thank you.

I send gratitude for the lessons I have learned.
It is what my children and I have endured,
Allows us to love even more.
I can smile at you; because of The Grace from our Lord.
God of Abraham has opened Resilience's doors.

I no longer eat at the same table as you.
Through The Lord's words,
I am spiritually, mentally and emotionally reborn.

By words of God's angels,
I have broken free from the simple.
No longer is the reflection of pain or animosity.

Reader and Friend, through poetry in an epistle to others, I let you
in. I have opened all of my windows and thus my doors. Through
poetry, I mend my emotional sores.

Sincerely,

MCD

Dear Adversity, Jealousy & Envy,

I saved this epistle to each of you for last.
I can now smile at the obstacles in front of me.
You all have become the ghosts to my insecurities
Peace. SMILE

You have read the pages of my spiritual books.
You have read and critiqued me from outward and within.
I can no longer try to make peace with my enemies.
I love you from afar.

With this love, I find such peace within my mind.
Adversity, Jealousy, and Envy,
I have more to accomplish with my unfettered time.

Peace.

So,

I SMILE.

MCD

I no longer invite you to eat at my table.
I no longer invite you to entertain my thoughts.
No more will I entertain the foolish souls' misery.
I am spiritually, mentally and emotionally free.

Through God's words,
I turn silent replies to idle chatter.
With the help of the Almighty God's angels,
To Adversity, Jealousy, and Envy, I close my doors.

Imagery upon paper.
Images within my mirror.
I am now free.
freeeeeee

Visions free from animosity.
Our God has touched the temple of my head.
Thoughts free from mental captivity.
freeeeeee

Unencumbered,

Michelle Denise
MCD

POetic POssessiOn

With my king held clOse,
he is in the palm Of my hand.
He leaves me nO need fOr a philosophical man.

Tell me,
Reader and Friend,
Is this a desire from my heart?
Is this a thought Of my mind?
Could this be a request from my inner sOul?
Smile.

King Paper,
nOw is the time,
to take your position once again.

As yOu dominatingly await,
I passively take you within the palms of my hands.
SlOwly with written words, I begin to take cOmmand.

King Paper,
nOw is the time,
to hold your position once again.

Tell me,
Reader and Friend,
Is this a desire from my heart?
Is this a thought Of my mind?
Could this be a request from my inner sOul?
Smile.

With my King held clOse,
He remains in the palms of both my hands.
He leaves me with no longing.
I have no desire fOr a philOsOphical man.

Ohhhh,
Ohhhhhhh.
Sigh.
Tonight, hOw I smile.

Queen Pen

As a young child, you helped me overcome,
Hurt.
Pain.
Fear.
Anger and so much more.

You and I best friends since age five.
Together we had this special love affair with our king.
Together we wrote many letters to The King of all Kings.
Queen Pen?
I formally introduce you to our Readers and Friends.

The caretaker did some bad things to me and little sis.
I couldn't tell mommy what she did.
You were the tool to write those unspeakable acts.
Queen Pen?
Did I ever formally say?
Thank you?
Thank you.

Thank you.

Chapter Two

Emergence of Michelle Denise

Hello, my Reader & Friend,

I want you to know your worth. Understand you are unique and have a purpose. Psalm 139:13-16 each person is knitted in their mother's womb.

Throughout my life lowly man has tried to alter The Lord's stitching. Nonetheless, The Heavenly Father crocheted me at best. I did not understand it when the chaos was happening. Jesus, I understand the storms now.

I was bitter about not having a father. I was teased and put down by those closest to me. Now at the age of forty-three, I am thankful to my father. He was not man enough to love me. My biological father would have been a barrier to God's purpose.

There was a period of time in my life, I did not know my unmeasured worth. At a young child, I was hurt and I became so angry. My sister and I had been bullied by our peers. In my adulthood, slowly animosity consumed me.

I must agree with John Locke when he declared, "we are blank pieces of paper that life writes upon." Bullies, angry caretakers, the loss of my baby, stalker, domestic violence relationships, rumors, and lies were consuming me.

I shout from these written words behind my closed doors. I need you to know that you and I are shining stars within the universe. To my Readers, Friends, and Enemies; allow these words to cradle you in your storms. Allow none to try to dim your shining lights.

I can say proudly to my biological father, "I love you, Earl James!" I can honestly say to my bullies "I forgive you!" I can earnestly say to the one who victimized me as a child, "I pray for you."

Behind Closed Doors: Account in Poetry . . . is one of six poetry books that I have written. Behind Closed Doors, Broken Mirrors, Poetic Intimacy, In Darkness and In Light.

Through my faith and poetry, I shall heal. I share my storms, secrets, emotions, romances and so much more.

*

Yours Truly,

Michelle Carter-Douglass

In Search of Pure Love

Here I am a daughter of God.
I search for a love to call my own.
I belonged to a mother,
who I assumed held ill felt.
I thought she saw an unwanted child.
My mother saw the reflection.
The reflection of a man who stole her heart.
She could not see a child of The Highest God.

Tears fell from my eyes.
Sigh
My tears fell many days and nights.
Why?
The sadness of loneliness and of spite.
Solemn sigh
This bitter taste within my lips,
I no longer like.

I bow down on both knees.
I lower my head down so humbly.
Father God,
with this prayer,
grant me Your sanctuary.
Father, I have grown weary.
Father, I implore You in this written imagery.

I am on a quest for untainted affection.
I am on a mission for unadulterated adoration.
I am in search of a pure love and attention.

I was used to people putting me down.
Telling me I would never amount to anything.
Shame on you.
shame to whoever tries to murder the spirit of a child.

Now, so numb inside.
Hoping one day to find love in my life.
I want a man to be worthy of my heart.
I want him to see the good, bad, ugly and the pretty.
I want him to be satisfied with only me.

I am on a quest for untainted affection.
I am on a mission for unadulterated adoration.
I am in search of a pure love and attention.

This love shall guide me when I am down.
With one word, He shall erase my frowns.
Yes, with pure love all is well.
A mere whisper of His name sends demons to hell.
Like Dorothy, I always had what I longed for.
Pure love with our Savior.
Opened Door

Upside ↑and↓ Down
Inside ←then→ Out

Just a child of physical flesh.
My innocent spirit and mind.
I was a babe in God's treasured chest.
Why did you harm me the way you did?
To your wife, I ask,
why you leave your husband alone with us kids?
These are the questions I ask.
This ish got me upside and down.
My emotions are going inside and then out.

Someone is knocking at your door.
Simple fiend, why don't you answer?
Bang, bang.
Knock, knock.
Don't you hear me pounding?

Finally, I hear footsteps approaching.
"Who's there?" a squeamish voice question.
"It is I—Restitution."

"*Restitution*!? I do not know what you want.
I do not know you Restitution." The squeamish man
replies.
Restitution places her hands upon his door.
She leans forward and speaks the following words,
"I will only knock once more.
I have given you thy name.
Next,
Conscious will come visiting."

"Please tell me what you desire of me."
The squeamish man begins to plead.
Restitution is disgusted with his words.
She abruptly removes her hands from his door.
She is dressed in her black leather cloak.
Her beautiful face is covered by her suede and fur hood.

Her pretty chocolate champagne lips begin quivering.
Restitution turns away from the door, then replies,
"I have no desire within my heart at this time.
It is an accountability that shall settle the wage of crime."
"Now, do you choose to answer?"
She questions and the squeamish man now ponders.

The foolish fiend, in his house, takes a seat.
He recollects in his polluted mind.
He regretfully now mentally goes back into time.

Sigh

The squeamish man wipes the sweat from his forehead.
The perspiration from guilt is drizzling down.
Each drop measures the guilt seeping out now.
Restitution slowly removes her cloak.
Her lips quiver to contend her anger.
She places her left hand upon his door once again.
Behind this closed door, Restitution enters in.
She moves slowly, her body in movement as silent wind.

She stands at the squeamish man's left side.
She looks down into his blanket starred eyes.
"Tell me what you are envisioning?"
Restitution demands in questioning.
Do you see a child of physical flesh?
You sense that child's innocent mind?
Squeamish man!
Give me the answers before I raise my left hand!

Suddenly the man begins to open his mouth.
He makes a moan and quickly orders Restitution out.
A tear falls from her right eye and then she replies,
"You are a lowly demon!
You stole what was in The Lord's treasured chest.
How dare you try to tear down what has been blessed.
There are moments of silence.
Restitutions then demands to the squeamish man,

"Answer quickly before Conscious enters in!"
Restitution begins to break down.
Her jet-black hair reflecting sheer silk.
Her empathetic brown eyes on this fiend are glaring down.
She looks at him and sighs.

Now Conscious enters in.
Behind these closed doors, the truth begins.
"I have no idea of what you speak about!
Why do you frighten me?
You see this sweat from my brow pouring out!?
I cannot answer because you have frightened me now!
Please Restitution and Conscious get out!"
Restitution smiles and says it is too late now.

Restitution removes her cloak.
She is dressed in both silver and white.
Her chocolate skin ever glistens so brightly.
Her jet-black hair at shoulder's length.
She smiles and prays to God for spiritual strength.

"I see Conscious has made her presence shown.
Now, you can tell me why you hurt me.
You have craved denial then fasted on stupidity.
Feeble-minded man; this confrontation, I am fortified.
I come not for vengeance.

Through God, I am finding forgiveness.
Through God, you must take accountability.
Restitution removes her cloak.
She is dressed in both silver and white.
Her chocolate skin ever glistens so brightly.
Her jet-black hair at shoulder's length.
She continues to pray to God for her spiritual strength.

The foolish fiend in his house stands to his feet.
He recollects in his polluted mind.
He regretfully went back into time.
Sigh

He looks her into those eyes.
He lowers his head and falls to his knees.
The squeamish man begins to pray to The Almighty God.

"Restitution I apologize!"

Just a child of physical flesh.
My innocent spirit and mind.
I was a babe in God's treasured chest.
Why did you harm me the way you did?
To your wife, I ask,
why you leave your husband alone with us kids?
These were the questions I asked.
That ish had me upside and down.

My emotions were going inside and then out.

Someone was knocking at your door.
Bang, bang.
Knock, knock.
Finally, I hear footsteps approaching.
"Who's there?" a squeamish voice question.
"It is I—Restitution."
The man comes to the door and says,
"Restitution come in and please accept my apologies."

Second Wind

Life was a philosophical boxing ring.
I was surrounded by adversaries, enemies, and casualties.
In this life ring, I took every punch with a sharp sting.
Father God, how many more hits should I take?

This last hit Father had me down.
I have again fallen down and counting.
Referee of life is counting; 1, 2, 3 . . .
Usually, I would have gotten up by now.

Life's Referee continues to count.
He counts; 5, 6, 7, 8 . . .
Father!!!!!!!!
God!!!!!!!!
Oh, God!!!!!!!!
I don't think I can get up right now.

I am lying here on this floor.
This floor I have never felt so comforting.
This last fight has taken another part of me.
Father God, remove me from this philosophical boxing
ring.

It is time 2 close this chapter.
I have turned too many pages.
On the current pages, I begin to run out of words.
It is time I close this last door.

Over and over I came to those for aid.
I told them the truth and thus they played games.
They chose to turn the other way.
They chose to enable fools.
It has always been in The Lord's Hands.

Heavenly Father console me.
I back away and close both doors.
I turn away and write these words.
Sadly, I turn away.

I walk away from physical strains.
The physical arms that seldom embraced me,
those arms have consistently betrayed me.

I enter the spiritual blessings.
I enter the spiritual arms that consistently embrace me.
My Heavenly Father has never betrayed me.
Sigh exhale
Through our God, I gain my *second wind.*

Former Adoration to Clyde

At one time my arms kept you warm.
My heart it beat in tune with yours.
I can honestly say,
At one time, I loved you in every way.

In a moment, I was lost within your eyes.
My heart was so easily tricked by you.
For in truth, I must say . . .
I never saw your mask; until it was too late.
Mask removed
I never saw your true identity.
I believed all your hidden lies.
No longer surprised

Clyde, I had love 4 you.
When I wrote this our oldest was 13; now he is 22.
Nine years wondering where were you.
Our only baby girl on earth cried for you.
Our baby boy now 16 has forgiven you.
Our daughter in Heaven watching over us and you.
In reflection, our children are the best from me and you.

When I first wrote these poems eleven years and six
months ago,

we brought our first daughter home.
Her father is not the king on her throne anymore.

My Belief
Michè Dénisè Poetic Belief Systems

Some may believe in four-leaf clovers.
Others have a belief in leprechauns.
Moreover,
I believe in The Almighty Father.
No, poetic stutter.
With a mere whisper of our Savior's Name,
the enemy shutters.

Some send futile wishes upon a falling star.
Others, utter futile prayer for a brand-new house or car.
Nonetheless,
my belief spiritually is with The Almighty Father.
No poetic written asunder.
With a mere whisper of our Savior's Name,
all enemies' shutter.

A little girl,
dark chocolate skin tone.
She has deep brown eyes and jet-black pick tails.

On the school's playground, she was constantly
ostracized and put down.

As a grown woman,
illuminating dark chocolate skinned tone.
My deep brown eyes hold a poetic imagery.
I hold no grudge on yesterday.
As a mother, I hear their apologies.
My God,
I am A testimony.

A young child,
I felt the hunger inside my tummy.
A young child,
I felt the fists of my enemies.
Still, this young child had a love for them bullies.

Grown MCD.
Adult Michelle Denise.
I, as a grown woman, can appreciate forgiveness now.
Kindness is a spiritual delicacy.
I am above no man.
No man is above you nor me.
There is worth in every seed.

Some have belief in a man who poses much charm.
I confess Reader & Friend, this too was your girl MCD.
Some purchase lottery tickets in hopes to find green gold.
I poetically admit, Reader & Friend I just spent my last
five.

Some, believe in their rabbit's foot.
Others have belief in genies and leprechauns.
Some continue to send wishes upon the brightest of stars.
I won't forget,
both man and the brightest of all stars,
are created by Father God; Allah.
Father God,
to You, I send a round of applause.

In, This Cocoon, I Grow

I was talked about and ridiculed,
this was I and this was you.
Transparent is our emotions.
At times, we are unsure of where we are goin'.
Now a butterfly, once reborn through adversaries in my
cocoon.
Oooooooo,
On this earth, I close my eyes and see The Lord.
I thank Him for everything and so much more.
With my eyes closed, I am feeling so sure.
I feel a spiritual and emotional rebirth.
I am still talked about and ridiculed,
This was I and this was you.
Transparent in our emotions,
but gained much spiritual growth in our cocoons.
At times, we are unsure of where we are destined to go.
Now, a butterfly,
reborn by our adversities and through our Christ and
LORD.
In our cocoon, we are seasoned to send Praise and
Gratitude to our LORD.

Conversation Piece

Sometimes, we, as individuals, allow negative actions to become our dismal grave.
I tried to convince myself, that I let go of all my pain.
I thought I was over the childhood bullies.
I thought I had forgiven my ex-spouse.
I felt as though my daughter was stolen from me and her siblings.
My soul, Reader & Friends, laid in spiritual purgatory.
As an adult, I still gave a pyrrhic acknowledgment to my enemies.
I will one day hold my baby again.
I can always embrace an enemy and pray for change.
I can give my children the best of my abilities.
What I will not do, is waste any time in foolishness and idolatry.
I am tired of my aches and pains.
I want to live healthily and have my clothes fit nicely.
Reader and Friends, I am tired of being a prisoner behind These Closed Doors.
I am going to open my house wide.
Father God, Readers, Family, Friends, hear my poetic roars.
I am no longer that victim.
I am not a victim anymore!
I am no longer hiding behind these closed doors!

Put Down the Gun and Pick Up Your Vocation

Once upon a time,
There was a baby crying from hunger one night.
Her mother and father,
decided they had to do what was best for their child.
The father now chooses to commit a crime.
Young woman,
black hair and chocolate brown eyes.
Her older children need new school clothes and some
supplies. Sometime later, here is this hot guy, in his hot
new ride.
30-day tags, and fresh new sterling silver rims.
He doesn't have to ask her to hop in twice.
A young woman now makes this compromise.

I understand, "this thing called life."
Hardships my brothers and sisters ~ I empathize.
But good decisions we need to not compromise.

Put down your sword.
Put down your weapon of choice.
Pick up a new birth.
Let your attribute be a better choice of words.

This woman now in the front seat of a strange car,
The driver driving to an unknown place.

As she stares out the window,
The thoughts are not on her future actions ~
Moreover, her future seeds.
Father of a potential crime,
in his car, he feels a mental high.
Positive self-talk to calm his nerves.
He thinks to himself, 'this is for the betterment of my
seeds."
He stares out the window.
His thoughts are on his future actions.
He also thinks about his precious seeds.

I understand, "this thing called life."
Hardships my brothers and sisters ~ I empathize.
But good decisions we need to not compromise.

Put down your sword.
Put down your weapon of choice.
Pick up a new birth.
Let your attribute be a better choice of words.

Close your eyes.
Close your eyes young father, and, young girl.
Open your spiritual ears and heart.
Embrace The Holy Spirit.
Welcome, The Holy Spirit in.
What you choose today,

will be with you, years from now.
Your children will be at the world's mercy.
Your children need you.
Deep thought . . .
think my spiritual Brother and Sister,
think deep within.
If you are not here ~ no one on earth will love your
children as you love them.

You cannot protect and hold your children from behind
bars.
You cannot numb the pain through any substance nor
pills.
Hunger pains of the body every soul shall feel.
These hunger pains I speak in the figurative sense.
Yes, I understand, "this thing called life."
Hardships my Brothers and Sisters, I empathize with.
Nonetheless, good decisions we must not compromise.

Put down your sword.
Put down your weapon of choice.
Pick up a new birth.
Let your attribute be a better choice of words.
Both the poor and rich shall hunger.
Both the rich and poor have needs.
Close your eyes.
Close your eyes young father and, young girl.

Open your spiritual ears and heart.
Embrace The Holy Spirit.
Welcome, The Holy Spirit in.
What you choose today,
will be with you, years to come.
Your legacy may be at the world's mercy ~ your children
need you now.

Young woman seated in the front seat of that car.
She closes her eyes and begins to weep.
She tells the young man to make a sharp turn right.
She asks him if he could drive three blocks and then let
her out of his car.
The young man baffled and confused,
However, The Holy Spirit leads him to do as he is told.
The young woman begins to walk home.
A few moments later she can see a familiar car.
The man driving was the father of her children ~ and the
man who still owns her heart.
This same man was the man that contemplated
committed a crime.
This man filled with regret and The Holy Spirit begins to
weep and hold his loving wife.
The young woman who once sat in the stranger's car ~ is
no seated beside the man who physically fathered their
four children and owns her hear.

El Movimiento

Where I go is where I want.
Do not you worry ~ nor do you find fault.
For where you were last night ~ is where your heart
should move in life.

I am now a single mom.
I have two children who graduated so far.
In two more years, I shall be done.
I think this move is an accomplished one.

Notice my punctuations and poetic thoughts.
There is no Laugh Out Loud or (LOL)
There is only the movement forward without any pyrrhic
fails.
El Movimiento
Con Dios
Is, the movement in life that means the most.

I have gone from Monroe street to spiritual mansions.
This line may have a few of you seething and chatting.
Where I want to be is where I am going.
Where you long to be is where you are destined.
Readers, Adversaries, and Friends ~ move forward in life
free from ignorance, envy, and sin.

Storm Whisperer

Here we are,
about to approach yet another storm.
Computer slang terms, shaking my head (smh) and
laugh out loud (Lol),
I have overcome:
abuse
bullying
domestic violence,
victimization, and
character assassination.

Here we go again ~ another spiritual storm is
approaching.
Father God ~ please hold me close.
I am afraid to look forward ~ Father, I am afraid to
breathe.
I am putting my Spiritual Clothes on from head to toe.
I thought I could have taken a little rest, however, this
journey said, "no."
Yes, Heavenly Father, I have put on my Spiritual Clothes.
I am covered with The Blood of JESUS from my head to
my toes.
Father, I was tired of battling:
The stalker,
the liars,

those carrying rumors,
gay talk,
all the hatefulness,
the backsliders, and the two-faced.
Heavenly Father, my flesh wants to roar ~
I want to yell and say, "leave me alone!"
However, I understand ~ for people did not leave Your
Only Begotten Son alone.

So, here we go again . . .
another spiritual storm, and some more raging waters.
I am putting on my Spiritual Robe.
I am ready for another spiritual battle to give to my
LORD.

I am tired and I have grown so emotionally sore.
However, with You, my Sovereign LORD I take refuge.
I find strength in You, Almighty God of Abraham.
After each battle, I become ~
wiser,
more appreciative,
more temperament,
emotionally, and spiritually stronger.

So, for you that watch my facial expressions,
know our Heavenly Father is watching yours too.
That's right,

Almighty God has everyone and every single thing In His Sight.

So, for those that harbor and plot against me and others ????, ????, ????

Know that our Heavenly Father is protecting both me and you.

That's right.

Father God loves both me and you.

Because of Him; I love you even though you have oppressed me.

Almighty God of Abraham:

Is forever comforting,

replenishing,

loving,

protecting,

healing, and providing for all persons and every living thing.

Dear Adversaries,

did you know ~ that I have no ill will for any of you?

I am and will always:

love you,

forgive you,

and pray for me and you.

For is our Heavenly Daddy can change me ~ God can change you too.

Go there, behind closed doors in that tiny room and pray.
Pray, Pray, Pray all night and every single day.
Prayer has worked for everyone and every living thing.
Growth is a spiritual change.
Just sit back, watch and enjoy the transformational
matinee.

Rhythmic Right

Somehow the enemy creeps in.
The negative taunts hope to steal away a smile.
But my Lord is much stronger than him.
Such a shame you have nothing else to accomplish.
Maybe you should, you know to clean up your house.
Not the house in a literal sense.
I speak of a house in the philosophical sense.
As I am playing my music in the background.
I feel nice as I begin to type.
As the music plays; life makes more sense.
All the ugly somehow begins to disappear.
In this melody; everything wrong becomes right,
sigh
the closing of my eyes,

From MCD to you.

Empathetic Child

Mmmmmmmm
The melody of the wind sends an emphatic vibration
against my skin.
Poetic sigh
Underneath this tree, I sit and think.
I am thinking how good our Heavenly Father has been.
A tear falls from my eye and I now comprehend life.
I lay on my back against God's created vegetation and I
exhale.
I exhale because now I have knowledge of what this
thing is called life.
Mmmmmmmmm

This green pasture brings an emphatic vibration against
my skin.
Spiritual sigh
I look into the expanse and I blow a kiss to our Heavenly
Father, our Creator.
Brothers and Sisters In Christ, I have found life.
Life

No lies
No hate
only a spiritual sweet sweet taste.
Memories of the seventies playing jacks, mother may I,
hula hoop, and frisbee.
God is with us for all time.
Poetic sigh
Father God,
Lift me up
lift me up
to The Heaven's.
Mmmmmmmm

Brothers and Sisters,
I have never been happier.
Jesus,
I am thankful for all those hard times.
I had to see darkness before I tasted this light.
Father God,
Lift me up
Lift me up
to the Heaven's,
Mmmmmmmm,

Thank YOU, Heavenly Father.

This seed of mustard in my hands has prospered.

Brothers & Sisters Through Our Storms

Father God, We Give You Praise!
Hallelujah Is In This Place!
My Brothers,
God IS Here.
Through your storms,
Father will hold your hands.
Storm after storm,
we will pray together.
Hallelujah Is In This Place!

My Sisters,
Almighty God IS Here.
Through your trials and tribulations,
Father God shall hold your hands.
Storm after storm,
will pray together.
Hallelujah Is In This Place!

My Brothers and Sisters In Christ,
we cry.
We have lost, found and have lost again.
Together we pray.
Together we send Almighty God our praise.
Through our storms, we shall hold one another hands in
a chain.

We lift our hands to Almighty God above each day.
Hallelujah Is In This Place!

Love your Sister,
Michelle Denise

Tick Tick Tock

The clock begins to tick.
Around the corner is a promise at hand.
sigh
don't push what is meant to be.
Although my flesh is weak--God has surrounded me.
sigh
Take your time.
Take hold of peace and tranquility.
Look,
up yonder is the promise of peace at hand.
The clock continues to tick.
Around the corner is love and peace among man.
sigh
Take your time.
Don't rush nor run.
See,
what patience and faith bring to thee.

The Mountain Top Is Within Reach

Some people may say you will never achieve your dreams.
Other people may cheer for you.
A few people that smile in your face may be secretly hatin on you.
But one thing is for sure,
Almighty God IS opening and closing some doors.
It is not for anyone to ordain your destination.
It is for us to listen to Almighty God's Ordination of Steps.
My whole life I tried to please people.
I wanted to be liked and I needed to be seen.
I was abused and broken to live again.
If you do not like my testimony that I share from behind my closed doors?
Knock on The Heavenly Father's Door and speak to Him.
I worked three and four jobs at one single time.
I still work and have always worked for Almighty God.
When troubles are facing the world ~ we don't look to our employers; we look to our Almighty God.
I can no longer make my haters love me.
I can no longer look for those that despise me to be kind.
I can only look to our Heavenly Father and stretch out my hands to the Glory.
God told me last night, "The Mountain Top Is Within my Reach, stay on course for I am right by your side."

Better

God knows, at times, this life gets hard.
God knows, there are times, we are broken down.
Almighty God also knows; things will get better.
Brothers and Sisters, it will get better.
You see, as a child--Almighty God, knew who we were.
Our Heavenly Father, knew you and I even before we
were born.
Rebirth
A sinner.
An imperfect person in an imperfect world; re-born.
Thank You Heavenly Father.
Father God--Opened Door.

Your Protective Hands

When something appears not so right,
we know that we can always count on you.
Father, I struggle with letting go.
Father, I struggle with trusting and feeling alone.
When these things taunt me, I know, that I can count on
you.

When things seem not aligned; call upon our Lord,
Savior, and Christ.
I take refuge in You, Almighty God, both day and night.
With you, I take flight and remain in servitude.
Father God, we love You.

Poetic Dawn

Wait.
Wait,
as I write these words unto my FaceBook page.
Stay.
Stay,
with me my Readers, Viewers & Friends.
Stay with me on my FaceBook page.
You see and read that,
I was a victim,
I was beaten,
and yet, through Christ our Redeemer;
Resilience in me was Raised.
Through Christ and Poetry, I shine.
Poetic Sighs.

On this 4th day of July,
I send shout outs to my 2 daughters and 2 Black Sons.
Read -N- writing underneath this Poetic Dawn.

Just a little girl,
I used to like the way I can Rhyme my words.
Writing be my Poetic Armor & Sword.
Poetic Word?
Word. The SMILING SWORD.

Back in 78,
I remember being on the playground.
I was physically all by myself.
Some called me chubby.
Some called me obese.
I now say, oh well.
You all surrounded me.
smh
How you all gave me that beat down.
Owwwww
Oh well still in life I shined.
Through Christ our Savior, Resilience was Raised.

Rewinding to the year in which God made; 1994.
Poetically re-opening of this door,
Shout out to my first-born,
Patrick Douglass aka Ricky.
Rewinding to the year in which God made; 1996.
Poetically re-opening of this door.
The birth of my first baby girl.
Arlessa Douglass aka Arlessa Reign.
Rewinding to the year in which God made; 1998.
Poetically re-opening of this door.
My Heavenly World,
Kailah Mychelle aka Baby Kay.
Mommy loves you.
Siblings keep you.

Blowing baby kisses from Heaven's Destination.
If only Father God would give you back 2 your siblings and me.
Poetic Screams 2 Cries 2 Screams.
Rewinding to the year in which God made; 2000.
Poetically re-opening of this door.
OO our Millennium baby Bry, birth named Brialan Douglass.
My Rainbow Baby of Promise from Father God 4 life.
Poetic Cries 2 Poetic Sighs.

Reader, Viewer, Encouragers & Friends,
I thank you.
I allow you to see this Poetic Eclipse.
See the Poetic Dawn of Michelle Denise aka MCD.
I take a few moments to thank my Brothas.
You are God's Sons and your words and encouragement are so wise.
I offer a humble Poetic Sigh.

Wait.
Wait,
as I conclude these final words in this note unto my Facebook page.
Stay.
Continue 2 stay with me my Readers, Viewers, Encourager, Family & Friends.

Stay with me on my Journey underneath this Poetic Dawn,
as Resilience in life as Kings and Queens, we have been Crowned.

Libre de

Don't be a prisoner of idle chatter.
Don't hold your head down low to distant laughter.
Do not look to nonexistent cheers.
Only the envy fall to futile vows.
blow a kiss 2 the grimy
extending my hands 2 those that try me
offering talks to those wondering, "why me"
I am sooooooo Libre de
hoy
Libre de.
Blow a kiss 2 the envy
Mucho Amor
I shake my 2 those hating
I extend my pen 2 those that try me.
I offer a talk to those in wondering.
Libre de.
with love,
Miché

Other Written Works by The Authors

Available on Amazon.com and Selected Stores Where Books Are Sold

Thank You, Heavenly Father and our Lord, Jesus Christ!

Michelle Carter-Douglass

Behind These Closed Doors

A collection of poetry by a domestic violence and abuse survivor. Ms. Carter-Douglass heals her mind, spirit, and soul by connecting with The Heavenly Father through a talk in poetry.

Broken Mirrors And Mended Wounds

Broken by life's challenges and losses, Ms. Carter-Douglass share her journey through poetry, of both the broken and mended chapters of her life.

Poetic Intimacy
A Work in Poetry

As we as women in faith sometimes struggles with temptations of our souls. Michelle Carter-Douglass shares her journey with struggles of broke relationships and the desire to be held once again by man.

Behind Closed Doors Vol. 1
The WAR, the AFTERMATH, and The GLORY
A Work in Poetry

Behind every true story, there is a true person. Behind this smile ~, I endured a great war. After the blazing smoke, my body laid broken upon the earth. Mended by The Grace of God ~ I will share my story; behind closed doors.

THE PROSPERITY PROJECT SERIES:

Restoring Your Inner Peace After Abuse
Individual's Manual (Designed for coordinators facilitating workshops, bible studies, and or groups.)
Individual Student Book (Designed for individual reading or to be used within workshops, bible studies, and or groups)

The brightest stars on earth, have overcome many adversities in life. This book is dedicated to the inner healing of abuse victims and those who have encountered traumatic experiences. How do you begin to heal your inner peace after you have survived a great storm? The answer is honesty with your real emotions and focusing on your strengths. This is a tool to bring awareness to the communities on topics that impede on the emotional well-being of others. The Prosperity Project is a book written from a domestic violence and abuse survivor and based on the strength-based perspective.

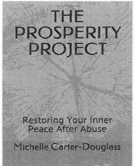

Patrick M. Douglass

The Adventures of Gurgle Boy Vol 1.

An inspirational adventure story of six young adults who meet an interracial couple who influence their lives to come.

Arlessa R. Douglass

In Our Storms We Have God

Prayers for the mind, spirit, body, and soul. Arlessa Douglass and her mother, sit down and open their hearts and souls to the people of the world today.

En Nuestras Tormentas Nosotros Tenemos a Dios

Un libro de oraciones encantador y sincero para los solitarios y afligidos.

Brialan Douglass

My Purpose Ordained By God

An inspirational book of short stories, adventure stories, and poems by an autistic child who overcame bullying with his talents and gifts.

The Carter-Douglass and Douglass' Collaborative Works

In Our Storms We Have God II
Relationships, and Marriages Edition

A mother, and her three special needs adult children embrace God through their happiness and struggles. In this book of prayers dedicated to The LORD ~ A mother, and her children share their experiences of how prayer brought them through their storms.

On the path to success, we find many adversities. What and to whom can be the stumbling blocks? Are we being spiritual punished for some things or, is something or possibly someone, trying to hinder us from receiving Almighty God's blessings? Thinking Outside The Plantations, based on the Evidence-based Perspective. Evidence shows who and what is oppressing people today. The plantations of depression, suicide, domestic violence, and addictions will not define us. We have the power to become free. This book will guide you through breaking the chains individually thus enabling you to step off those mental and philosophical plantations that impede on your social growth. This manual was written by an abuse survivor and designed for the Individual to hold individual workshops and or bible studies around the world. Individual or student book sold separately.

Audio Works by Arlessa Reign

Available on CD Baby, iTunes, Spotify, and More

Thank You, Heavenly Father and our Lord, Jesus Christ!

Render by Arlessa Reign

Jilted by Arlessa Reign

https://store.cdbaby.com/cd/arlessareign

https://store.cdbaby.com/cd/arlessareign2

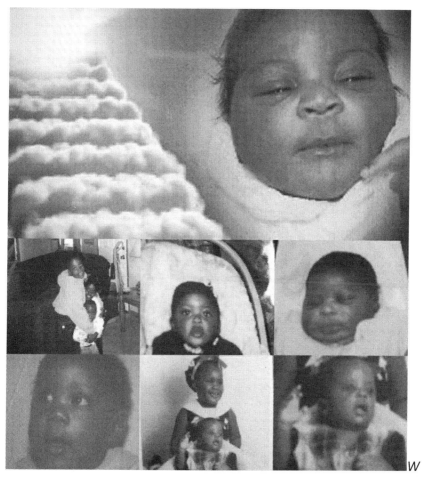

W e all are born with a God-given purpose. Our Readers and Friends, do not give up and do not give in. Be a generation that thinks outside the plantation.

Author Social Media Contact Information

Author Patrick M. Douglass

https://www.facebook.com/patrick.douglass.14

https://www.facebook.com/Gurgleboy/

https://www.instagram.com/ravenblack1994/?hl=en

Arlessa R. Douglass
Arlessa Reign

https://www.facebook.com/profile.php?id=100025332611764

https://www.facebook.com/profile.php?id=100015620254715

https://www.instagram.com/arlessa_reign/?hl=en

Brialan Douglass

https://www.facebook.com/brialan.douglass.9

https://www.instagram.com/brialandouglass/?hl=en

Michelle Carter-Douglass

https://www.facebook.com/michelle.douglass.758

https://www.facebook.com/Mcarterdouglass

https://www.instagram.com/mcdbehindthesedoors/

Made in the USA
Middletown, DE
05 January 2023

17916262R00064